Barcelona

Bess Wohl's other plays include *Grand Horizons* (Tony nomination for Best Play), *Small Mouth Sounds* (Outer Critics Circle Award), *Make Believe* (OCC Award), *Camp Siegfried*, *Continuity*, *American Hero*, *Barcelona*, *Touched*, *In*, *Cats Talk Back* and *Pretty Filthy* (Lucille Lortel and Drama Desk nominations for Outstanding Musical). Her plays have been produced at theatres in New York, around the US and internationally. Awards include the Sam Norkin Special Drama Desk Award, the Georgia Engel Playwriting Award, a MacDowell Fellowship and inclusion on Hollywood's Black List of Best Screenplays. Wohl is an Associate Artist with The Civilians, and an alumna of Ars Nova's Play Group. She has also written for film and television. She is a graduate of Harvard and the Yale School of Drama and lives in New York City.

by the same author from Faber

CAMP SIEGFRIED

BESS WOHL

Barcelona

faber

First published in 2024
by Faber and Faber Limited
The Bindery, 51 Hatton Garden
London, EC1N 8HN

Typeset by Brighton Gray
Printed and bound in the UK by CPI Group (Ltd), Croydon CR0 4YY

All rights reserved
© Bess Wohl, 2024

Bess Wohl is hereby identified as author
of this work in accordance with Section 77 of the
Copyright, Designs and Patents Act 1988

All rights whatsoever in this work, amateur or professional,
are strictly reserved. Applications for permission for any use
whatsoever including performance rights must be made in
advance, prior to any such proposed use,
to Olivier Sultan, CAA, 405 Lexington Avenue,
19th Floor, New York, NY 10174
olivier.sultan@caa.com, (212) 277.9000

No performance may be given unless a licence
has first been obtained

This book is sold subject to the condition that it shall not,
by way of trade or otherwise, be lent, resold, hired out
or otherwise circulated without the publisher's prior consent
in any form of binding or cover other than that in which
it is published and without a similar condition including
this condition being imposed on the subsequent purchaser

A CIP record for this book
is available from the British Library

ISBN 978-0-571-39542-2

Printed and bound in the UK on FSC® certified paper in line with our continuing
commitment to ethical business practices, sustainability and the environment.
For further information see faber.co.uk/environmental-policy

2 4 6 8 10 9 7 5 3 1

Barcelona received its European premiere at the Duke of York's Theatre, London, on 21 October 2024. The cast was as follows:

Irene Lily Collins
Manuel Álvaro Morte
Understudy Irene Manon Stieglitz
Understudy Manuel Jay Rincon

Director Lynette Linton
Set & Costume Designer Frankie Bradshaw
Lighting Designer Jai Morjaria
Composers & Sound Designers Duramaney Kamara & Xana
Video Designer Gino Ricardo Green
Wigs, Hair & Makeup Designer Cynthia De La Rosa
Intimacy & Movement Director Shelley Maxwell
UK Casting Director Heather Basten CDG
Associate Director Katie Greenall
Associate Set Designer Natalie Johnson
Associate Costume Designer Caroline Alice Stevens
Associate Lighting Designer Luca Panetta
Props Supervisor Charlotte King
Voice Coach Hazel Holder
Drama Therapist Wabriya King
Fight Director Kate Waters
Production Manager Kate West
Associate Production Manager Charlotte Ranson

Company Stage Manager Jonathan Stott
Deputy Stage Manager Anna Sheard
Assistant Stage Manager (Book Cover) Jinwen Chen
Head of Wardrobe Chris Cope
Wigs, Hair & Makeup / Wardrobe Deputy Lauren Osborne
Head of Sound Franny Lagemann
Deputy Head of Sound Vanessa Garber
LX Board Ops Donna Percival & Stephen Thompson

Characters

Manuel
Fifty-ish. Sexy. Elegant. Tall, dark and Spanish.

Irene
Young. American. A tourist.

Place

Barcelona

Time

Spring, 2009

BARCELONA

Note

/ denotes where the next character should begin speaking.

This playscript went to print while rehearsals were still in progress, so may differ slightly from the version performed.

A small apartment in Barcelona.

High windows that look out on an electric night sky and, from afar, the famous cathedral, La Sagrada Familia.

Cardboard boxes everywhere, as if someone is moving.

The key turns in the lock. A giggling, American woman bursts in, very drunk. Wearing only one shoe, a stiletto heel. This is Irene.

She is followed by Manuel, a Spaniard.

She throws herself at him with abandon. He responds, trying to keep up with her, stumbling as they go –

They move all around the apartment, desperate, clumsy, wild –

As things become more heated, she starts to giggle. It's a bit awkward. She giggles once. Twice. Three times and then –

Irene It's just that I never do this.

Manuel You mean –

Irene This! This. I mean, I never, *ever* –

Manuel It's okay?

Irene Oh yeah, no, it's okay, I'm good, it's good – I'm good to go –

She jumps on top of him.
 They continue.
 He removes his jacket, struggling a bit, and she gets a good look at him, seemingly for the first time.

Hi. You're cute.

Manuel Thank you.

Now she takes in the apartment.

Irene Oh my God, this is so cute! This is cute!

Manuel It is only small –

Irene Well yeah, but it's cute. It's really, really cute.

Manuel As I tell you, my primary house is in Madrid –

She gets on top of him, flirting.

Irene You know they say you really get to know a person, not from talking to them or whatever but from seeing where they live?

Manuel Who says that?

Irene They say it. Them.

Manuel Ah yes. Them. (*Flirty.*) Well, shall I show you how *I* really get to know a person?

Irene groans, giggles.

Irene Ooooh, okay, that's cute, that's really …

He pulls her to him again.

Wait wait wait. How do you say cute?

Manuel *Lindo.*

Irene (*as Manuel*) *Lindo.*

Manuel The tongue on the teeth like this.

Irene (*Spanish accent*) Like this?

Manuel *Lindo.*

Irene *Lindo.* How's my tongue?

Manuel Good. That's good. *Lindo* or you can say *linda* –

Irene Linda?

Manuel Masculine, feminine.

Irene No, it's just that, I have an Aunt Linda.

Manuel Really.

Irene She is not cute. Anyway. *Linda. Muy linda!* It's so Spanish. I really feel like I'm in Spain.

Manuel Because you are.

Irene Olé!

They continue to make out –
  As they do, she can't help glancing around the apartment with her eyes.

Cute curtains. Pottery Barn?

Manuel What?

Irene No, it's just, I think I saw these exact curtains in a catalogue somewhere.

She lifts her head, sees something out the window.

And oh my God, look! I think I saw that in the guidebook.

She might scamper over to see it.

Manuel Ah yes, La Sagrada Familia.

Irene I saw that in the guidebook and now it's right there, through a window.

Manuel Yes.

Irene Look at it. It looks *exactly* like in the guidebook. It looked better in the guidebook, actually.

Manuel That must be a really good guidebook.

She laughs.

Irene It is. (*In a Spanish accent, suave like him.*) It is a really good guidebook, a really good guidebook.

She starts to do a flirty, fun dance as she makes her way back to him.

(*Still in a Spanish accent.*) It is really, really good ... *Muy, muy, muy lindo* guidebook ... *Muy lindo* ...

Until –
Halfway through this dance, she trips and falls hard.

Manuel *Cuidado, cuidado!* (*In English.*) Careful.

She curls up in foetal position on the floor. Drunk and in pain.
Alarmed, he runs to her.

Ah, you are okay? Let me – let me help you, please –

He slowly helps her move to the sofa. She sits, doubled over, the alcohol hitting her hard.

Irene (*quietly*) I think I almost fell.

Manuel You are ... Are you ...

She leans back onto him.
Clutches him suddenly, making him into her security blanky.
Unsure what to do, he strokes her hair.

Are you all to be okay?

She closes her eyes.

Irene Oh yeah, yeah ... I'm all to be okay. I'm strong like bull. Grrrr. Did you know my ancestors literally *walked* across the United States of America? The pioneers? Ever heard of them?

Manuel Yes. I mean, not yours in particular, I don't think.

Irene We still have the quilts.

Manuel Wow.

Irene They took a boat all the way from England to America, this was like many generations ago, and they started in Virginia, and, like, okay, can you imagine walking from, like, Virginia to Utah? That's like, I don't know how well you know American geography? But that's, there's the whole middle part, the Midwest, the . . . Oklahoma, Indiana, the Dakotas – you hit a giant lake, you have to go around it, you hit one crazy mountain range, you have to completely turn back –

Manuel You already tell me this.

Irene What?

Manuel At the bar you already tell me this whole story.

Irene I did?

Manuel Step by step by step.

Irene Oh God, have I been talking too much? I'm like total diarrhoea of the mouth syndrome.

Manuel What?

Irene It's like, it's like, coming out of my mouth is, um . . . Streams of poo.

Manuel stares at her.
    It's awkward.

So.

Manuel So.

Irene What's a girl got to do to get a drink around here?!

Manuel You –

Irene Don't answer that. I know what you're thinking – you're so bad!

Manuel You should probably not have any more.

Irene Oh, come on –

Manuel Anyway, I have nothing, apologies –

Irene (*sing-song, cute and naughty*) I don't believe you . . .

Irene wanders, stumbles –

Manuel Please, careful –

Irene Ouch. Wait. (*Sees a bottle on a shelf.*) Oooh, what's that, over there – aha!

Manuel No, please. No. That is only saving, being saved, for the special occasion.

Irene Perfect. Tonight is the special occasion – the universe brought us together.

Manuel No, truly –

Irene And maybe tonight is . . . Let's pretend, okay? Let's pretend tonight is . . . Our last night on earth.

He looks at her.
Their eyes meet.

And we have nowhere to be. Nothing to do in the morning. And so maybe just . . .

She looks at him pleadingly.

One drink? *Un poco? Por favor? Que sera, sera?*

She starts to hum.

Manuel Don't. Please. Don't do that.

She hums a little more.
He relents, if only to quiet her.

Fine. One drink.

He takes the bottle, goes to get an opener.

Irene Do you guys really say that here? *Que sera sera?*

Manuel We can, yes.

Irene That's so cool. I love that. I love Spain. I wish I spoke Spanish. Is it the language of love? I think that's Italian. What's Spanish the language of?

He comes back.

Manuel Spain. And most of South America.

Irene Half of South America speaks Portuguese.

Manuel I did not say –

Irene You said 'most'. So, that's wrong. Technically. Just 'cause we're in Spain –

Manuel We are in Catalunya. People here speak Catalan. Technically.

Irene Yeah, okay, Bar*th*elona. I know, everything's '*th*'.

Manuel That's Castilian –

Irene (*ignoring him*) But who speaks Catalan? I mean, do you speak Catalan?

Manuel No. Because I tell you, I am from Madrid.

Irene Exactly. See? You totally just proved my point.

Manuel What was the point?

Irene You're a foreigner here too.

Manuel Okay.

Manuel pours them two glasses of wine.

Salud.

Irene *Salud.*

Manuel *Un brindis por nuestra última noche en la tierra.*

Irene (*no idea what he said*) Right.

Manuel You must look in the eyes.

They do.

Irene Okay wow. Hi. You are beautiful I think I need the bathroom.

Manuel Please. Yes. Right through this door.

She starts to go.
Then turns.

Irene Did something happen to my shoe?

Manuel You threw it at my head.

Irene (*surprised*) Oh.

She rushes off to the bathroom.
Alone, Manuel exhales.
He carefully sips his wine.
Savours it.
Considers the bottle.

(*Offstage.*) It's so cute in here. I love it.

Manuel slowly looks to where her voice is coming from.
He drinks down his wine.

(*Offstage.*) Uh – uh-oh.

Something CRASHES from the bathroom.

(*Offstage.*) I'm fine! I'm fine!

Irene appears at the bathroom door, looking a tad green.

Um, scusi?

Manuel Is there a problem?

Irene Um, it's just, the toilet, it's just maybe not . . .

Manuel Ah, yes, ah – I should have said – it's a bit stopped.

Irene I might have thrown up a tiny bit. And I peed.

Manuel Thank you.

Irene Sorry. It's just, I can't, like wash my mouth or my hands, 'cause the sink's all – the knob – I just got some rusty water in my mouth, it's –

Manuel I apologise, I forgot, all the water is off – I should have told you before –

Irene No, it's just, I'm normally extremely hygienic. Do you have water anywhere – / I think I need –

Manuel I apologise, here, have this Rioja.

He passes her a glass.

Irene How can you not have water?

Manuel I told you, my primary house –

Irene Okay, okay, I heard you – Madrid. But still . . . Go to the store, you know?

Manuel (*pointedly*) I wasn't expecting a guest.

Irene Fine.

She sips the wine.
  Makes a face.

Manuel Is okay?

Irene It tastes like puke. Sorry, I don't mean to be rude, but – (*Takes another sip.*) There. That's better. Huh. It's pretty good. Very 'fruit forward'.

Manuel This is what I am telling you, the real Spanish Rioja.

Irene Wait, so what were we having at the bar?

Manuel They serve cheap sangria to the tourists.

Irene Really? That's not nice.

Manuel They hate the tourists, mostly the English, also the Australians –

Irene Very not nice –

Manuel But, of course, they hate the Americans most –

Irene Wait. How could they tell I'm American?

Manuel Seriously?

Irene I could be Swedish. I could be Dutch.

Manuel No, you couldn't.

Irene Or, like, I have a friend who said, like, I should pretend to be *Canadian*. I was like, that's so boring. What's more boring than a Canadian? I mean, I am so tired of hearing about the Canadians with all their free everything. It's like, don't be so far north, you know, it's annoying.

Manuel You are quite clearly American.

Irene Well, I'm not sure if that's an insult.

Pause.
Manuel refills his glass.

Why are we talking about this!? We're having fun, right, Manolo? Wait, what happened to my shoe?

Manuel You threw it at my head.

Irene I know! *Problemo solvedo!*

She takes off her one shoe.
She walks around, looking at the apartment.
The sound of a siren from somewhere, far, far off in the distance.

So . . . Did you, like, forget to call the plumber? (*Off him.*) The bathroom?

Manuel As you can see. I am moving.

Irene Oh. But –

Manuel Tomorrow, in the morning, the movers come.

Irene Oh. Wow. You better get packed.

Manuel It's not so easy.

Irene Trust me, I know. It's like they say, they say there's like three really depressing things in life?

Manuel Only three?

Irene Yuh-huh. And they're, like, um . . . Death, divorce, and moving. Those are the three worst things in life. And I think they figured out that moving might be the most stressful of all of them actually. Anyway, that explains it. I was wondering what all the boxes were for.

Manuel Yes.

Irene I knew they weren't just decoration. That would be weird if they were. Like, 'We have these boxes here for decoration. They really add to the ambience.' Like, this year's trend! Boxes. I'm sorry. When I'm nervous I make dumb jokes. Not that I'm nervous, or, well, they're not even jokes, it's just like, dumb things like fly out of me. Just, like, out of my mouth. Not out of anywhere else – what am I talking about?

Manuel You are nervous?

Irene Should I be?

Manuel Not at all.

Irene I just don't normally, you know, with strange –

Manuel You came to me. In the bar. I was sitting in peace, yes, not bothering / anyone –

Irene You were fully staring at us.

Manuel You ask me, 'Are Spanish men better in bed?' I don't know. Better than what –

Irene No no no, that was a dare. From my girlfriends, it wasn't . . . We just thought you were cute. You're the one who brought me back to your place, which, hello, is clearly where you have sex with your mistresses.

He looks at her.

Manuel No.

Irene Come on. I heard all Europeans have mistresses.

Manuel You do not approve?

Irene Me?

She thinks.

In a way it's okay, I mean, if that's how you cope with the whole one person for the rest of your life nightmare of it all. I don't know, this is all way out of my comfort zone. I don't really drink, for starters. Plus, the jet lag. I mean, who even knows what time it even is in Denver. And a time change can really, like, fuck with your sense of self.

Manuel But it is good to have new senses, no?

Irene I guess. I don't know. I don't want a new sensation if it's, like, lying in a bucket of rats or something. But you seem really nice.

Manuel Good.

Irene looks at him for a beat.
She starts to laugh: nervousness, exhaustion, arousal.

What?

Irene No, I just – I was just thinking of this thing I saw on 20/20?

Manuel Twenty-twenty?

Irene It's like the news, but more interesting? Anyway, I saw this thing on 20/20 like a couple months ago, this scientist was saying that a woman gets more turned on by watching two *chimpanzees* have sex than by seeing a naked man if he isn't, you know, ready to go.

Manuel Which woman?

Irene I don't know, all women. Anyhoo, it's just a study, why am I talking about this –

Manuel It's okay, I already saw, at the bar –

Irene What, what did you see? Oh my God. What did you see?

Manuel The sex beads.

Irene Oh, no no no no, those were a joke! The anal beads – did you think we would – those were a joke! No, see, it's because, it's a bachelorette party. Well, it's a bachelorette weekend, so we give each other all this stupid stuff like penis whistles – that's a whistle, shaped like a, you know – nobody's ever going to *use* that stuff. We're just, you know, me and my girlfriends. Playing around. Why? Do you?

Manuel What?

Irene Do you use that stuff?

Manuel No. In Spain, we don't need the toys. We think lovemaking is enough.

Irene Right. That's cool. Well . . . Here there's this whole, I mean *there*, there's this whole, this whole ritual of, like, pre-wedding insanity. I mean, like, bachelor parties, with the strippers . . . I mean this guy I know, he actually, at his bachelor party, he actually ate a banana out of a stripper's you know, hoo-ha.

Manuel 'Hoo-ha'?

Irene Yeah, and then when his fiancée found out, that was my friend, she found a rubber in the trash because he had put the banana in a rubber, *thank God*, and the fiancée was like, 'What's going on? You ate a banana out a stripper's hoo-ha? I don't even know who you *are*.' Oh, I know, she was like mad, she was like –

She reaches in her bag and pulls out a small whistle shaped like a penis. Blows on it.
  Very loud.

Manuel (*covering his ears*) Ahhhhhh.

Irene (*overlapping*) You're under arrest! With my penis! You're under penis arrest!!

Manuel No, no more. No no no. Enough!

He roughly climbs on top of her, pinning her down.

Irene Oh, shit. I hope I didn't wake anybody up.

Manuel There is no one living here.

Irene No, but I mean, in the building.

Manuel There is no one in the building.

Irene Really? No, but I mean . . .

She wriggles away from him.

There's nobody? In the whole . . .

He shakes his head.
  Pause.

Why not?

Manuel pauses.
  It's hard to say what's next.

Why not.

Manuel Tomorrow. They destroy it.

Irene Destroy the . . .

Manuel looks around at all the things.

Manuel Terrible, right? It's so cute.

Irene It is sad. I mean . . . It's . . .

Irene looks around.

Why?

Manuel Why?

Irene Why do they destroy it?

Manuel They make a, how do you say . . . a . . . *centro commercial*. Commercial centre?

Irene A shopping mall?

Manuel Yes. That is only why I am moving.

Irene But . . . You said tomorrow? They're coming to tear this whole place down?

Manuel just stares at the things.

And you're not even packed?

Manuel (*gestures to the apartment*) Look.

Irene I know, no, it's just, 'cause, in America, they would probably not let you still be here right now.

Manuel This is not in America.

Pause.

Irene Wait. You don't hate Americans, do you, Manolo?

Manuel Manuel.

Irene Right. 'Cause honestly we're not so bad anymore. We have Obama.

Manuel Perhaps.

Irene What?

Pause.

Manuel No, nothing. It's . . . It's only your big cars, your big everything, your McDonald's –

Irene Well, I don't eat McDonald's. I hate McDonald's.

Manuel Your *imperialismo*, imperialism, yes – of course and your wars.

Irene Wars? What wars? Iraq? That wasn't just us, there was England, Spain –

Manuel But you started it.

Irene We started it? Hi, are we five? Are we five, really? You know, it's like, half the time it's like we're doing too much, leave the people alone. And then half the time it's like, send us more bombs – it's like, figure out what you want, people. It's a lot of responsibility, like, being in charge of the entire world, and so it's easy to just blame the Americans –

Manuel I never said it was easy –

Irene And anyway, we're getting out of Iraq.

Manuel But what do you leave behind?

Irene Saddam Hussein was a very bad guy, okay?

Manuel Okay, but still –

Irene He tortured people, he had them torn apart by animals – you have to agree that they're / better off –

Manuel I don't have to agree with anything –

Irene You don't agree the world is better off –

Manuel I don't believe you kill one hundred thousand innocent souls to get one evil man –

Irene And I think that's easy to say when you never had to deal with that evil man, when you live in freedom and safety –

Manuel We had terror attack.

Irene 9/11? I was *in New York when it happened*. I was in my hotel, and I saw it on TV. It was / so upsetting –

Manuel I speak of *Los Atentados del once M*.

Irene The . . .

Manuel You don't know. Of course, / you don't know.

Irene No, I do, I do know, that was the –

Manuel The train. Madrid. Atocha station.

Irene Oh, right, yeah, that was, that was awful.

Manuel One hundred ninety-one killed. Thousands wounded.

Irene And, remind me, who did it? What was the point?

Manuel What was the point? Good question.

Irene What I mean is . . .

Manuel It was all lies. First they tell us it's ETA. Basque separatists from up north?

Irene Right . . .

Manuel Then ETA says no, it was not us, we can't do something this big. We find out. The stupid president, Aznar, he is lying. He doesn't want us to know in fact it's Jihadists. Al Qaeda.

Irene But why would he lie about that?

Manuel Because if he told the truth, we would realise that it's all his fault. Because he shook hands with George Bush and followed America into your war.

Irene Not my war.

Manuel No, I know. Of course. Not your fault at all.

Irene Okay, you know what? Please don't say any more bad things about my people or species or whatever –

Manuel Okay.

Irene It's lame, it's practically cliché. We're all citizens of the world, here, okay? We live in a global situation.

Manuel I live in Madrid.

Irene Well, congratulations, but you know what? That doesn't make you better than me. Just 'cause you're European. 'Cause you 'know more about wine / than I do'.

Manuel That's not what I said.

Irene We don't need water, we have Rioja! And chorizo! And cheese! We eat dinner ridiculously late! We sleep all afternoon! We have small plates!

She takes a gulp of wine, getting on a roll.

Manuel Okay, this is enough –

Irene We don't have to change or sacrifice or move forward and join the future. But guess what? The future is where shit is happening. The future is what we're trying to cope with where I come from. But no, you sit back and relax with the rest of the, the Buena Vista Social Club – smoking cigarettes – newsflash, nobody smokes anymore –

Manuel Thank you –

Irene But sit there and do it, my friend, with your massive fucking hangover, blaming America and your president and the lies –

Manuel Who is sitting and blaming? Days after this attack, we have an election, we vote the president out, we get out of this war, *punto* –

Irene And that's exactly what the terrorists wanted, right? To influence your election, your foreign policy. So what did you do? You let the terrorists win.

Manuel (*with force, furious*) Enough. *Basta*.

Pause.

Irene Also, I have mace. Just so you know.

Manuel What is mace?

Irene It makes a, like, force field of protection if you spray it. It's bad. It could hurt you, for real.

Manuel I don't think so.

Irene It could. And I have it, right here, in my purse. Oh, shit, where's my purse? Have you seen my purse? (*Off his shrug.*) Did you steal my purse? Oh my God. Did you . . . You stole my purse?! I *knew* you would steal my purse. Oh my God, I knew it, I knew it, my friend warned me, she said, she said Canadians will fuck you up, you know, Canadians –

She looks around for her purse wildly.
She finds the one shoe that she was wearing before.

And where's my other fucking shoe?!

Manuel You threw it at my head.

Irene (*starting to totally freak out*) I knew it. I knew I shouldn't have come here with you – and oh my God oh my God I can't even mace you because my mace is –

Manuel In the bathroom.

Irene What?

Manuel Your purse is in the bathroom. You leave it there.

Irene starts to walk towards the bathroom.

Irene Don't try to trick me, fucker. We are very good at security. Like you would probably get the death penalty. We have that over there. In Texas.

Manuel Go look.

Irene Don't try any funny stuff.

She goes into the bathroom.
    Manuel lights a cigarette, calming his frayed nerves.
    He looks around the apartment.
    The boxes, the task ahead.

He is overwhelmed.
After a moment, Irene comes back with her purse, incredibly apologetic.
He looks up.

I'm sorry. I'm sorry I called you fucker.

Pause.

Also, just – everything I've said this whole night, about – Iraq and the pioneers and – just, can we just forget everything I've ever said? 'Cause, it's like, my dad's always like, 'Toughen up! You're pioneer stock!' like it makes me special or something but . . . What is he talking about? What am I talking about? I'm just going to stop talking, I'm sorry.

She takes a sip of wine.
Manuel considers this.

Manuel Okay.

Irene Also, one more thing, there's, um, you probably just shouldn't look in the toilet, because of the plumbing situation.

Manuel You said.

Irene (*genuine, pained*) I'm so so sorry.

Manuel I know.

Pause.

Irene I hope I didn't ruin the, like, ambience?

Pause.

I mean here I am in Spain with, like, a totally hot local Spanish guy from a tapas bar and we're drinking Rioja and I mean, if this isn't the ultimate romantic, like, you know, like *Dos Equis* guy fantasy? Do you guys have that commercial? It's, like, the beer's called *Dos Equis*, and there's a guy and it might be Mexican, anyway, the guy's like, 'Stay thirsty, my friends.'

Manuel Uh-huh.

Irene 'Stay thirsty, my friends.' It's funny, if you know what it is.

She roots in her purse for something.

Gum? It's all the way from Denver.

Manuel No thank you.

Irene It's Big Red. Do you have that here?

Manuel I don't think so.

Irene It lasts pretty long.

Irene puts a piece of gum in her mouth. Then another. She chews.

Oral fixation.

Manuel Congratulations.

Irene Thanks.
Anyway. I should go, I should let you pack –

Manuel (*suddenly vulnerable*) Don't go.

Irene (*surprised*) Oh. (*Then.*) Okay. Well. At least I should, I should, um, I should text my girlfriends and let them know where I am.

Manuel Yes, of course.

She grabs her phone.

Irene Where am I?

Manuel *Carrer de Sant Antoni Maria Claret, ochenta y uno B.*

Irene Did I, did we tell them where we were going before we left the bar?

Manuel You mean before you chased me out of the bar –

Irene I did not chase you –

Manuel And your 'friends' barely noticed?

Irene They were wasted. They have a drinking problem. Like, not each of them, but on the whole? Did you see how much they drunk? Drank? Drunked? What? I swear I went to college.

Manuel Drank.

Irene That's really sad. *Tu hablas* better *Ingles* than *mio*. It's true. You speak like, I mean, seriously, you could be American if we were, like, in New York.

Manuel *Gracias.*

Irene (*re: the phone, to herself*) Oh crap, I'm at three per cent. Okay, where are we?

Manuel *Carrer de Sant Antoni Maria Claret, ochenta y uno B.*

Irene Maybe you should type it into the . . .

Manuel If you wish.

He takes the phone.

Irene No funny business.

He gives her a look, then types it and hands the phone back to her.
She looks at it, no idea how to evaluate if it's right. A beat.

Okay, that looks good. (*She presses send.*) And now they know where I am.

A pause.
Suddenly, her phone rings to the tune of Beyoncé's 'Single Ladies'.

Manuel Do you need to answer?

Irene Nah, I'll call back. Actually, you know what? Let me just turn that off –

She goes to the phone. It stops.

Manuel Was it your friend?

Irene Who?

Manuel Who is getting married.

Irene Oh yeah. She's out being crazy, probably, you know, this is like our last hurrah. We're really into tapas.

Manuel Ah.

Irene And we're going to go, like, see flamingo, and all the Gaudí stuff, and basically, you know, bond.

Manuel Of course.

Irene 'Cause she's nervous I think 'cause it's, like, a big thing, it's just a really stressful thing actually. Because you look at your life, and you kind of think, okay, this is it. And that could be in a good way, you know, like, this is it! The fairy tale! Yay! Or that could be in sort of a sad way, like . . . This is it.

Manuel *(with empathy)* Yes.

She recovers.

Irene Yeah. So we all just wanted to, like, we all wanted to have like that one last totally crazy girls weekend and one of us, her dad has a plane, he's like, he has a football team too – you know American football not, like, your kind of football – so anyway, we all flew over together and then so hence me wasted at the tapas bar and hence me wasted here right now.

Manuel Wasted?

Irene Drunk. Doing shots. Whatever. It's stressful, you know. You gotta blow off steam.

She blows the penis whistle very softly. Smiles.

Are you?

Manuel What?

Irene Married.

Manuel Yes.

Irene Oh.

Manuel I apologise. I don't know you well enough to lie to you.

Irene It's okay.

Manuel My wife and I . . . We no longer speak.

Irene You mean . . .

Manuel She can't look at me any longer.

Irene Oh.

Manuel It happens.

Irene What? What happened? Never mind, it's none of my . . . Never mind.

He gives her a look – she's touched something very painful.

Manuel You really want to know?

Irene I mean, not if you don't want to talk about it, it's . . .

Manuel Only I don't want to scare you.

Irene You won't. I'm strong like bull. I'm like a bull at three per cent.

Manuel How can I describe it? In English.

He searches for the words.

Imagine someone touches you gently. You like it. It makes you feel safe. And warm, yes? This touch. It's everything.

Irene Okay.

Manuel And then you feel, in the touch, maybe a little, how do you say, the fingernail? Like a scratch. A little, tiny scratch. It still feels good, yes? It's a nice feeling. They know you, these hands. They know how to find all the places you like.

Then the scratching, it starts to slowly lift a little bit of skin. Tiny traces of your skin, slowly so you don't even notice but soon the skin is pink. It feels hot. A little sting, from time to time, but it's okay, you let it go.

Then, each thing that happens in life, because many things happen in life, the hands grip you harder. The nails go in. You want to be iron, strong, you wish to be leather and steel, but the armour is not impenetrable.

The hands get through. The nails dig down in your skin, into your veins. Rip into your muscle and scrape on your bone. They snap your fingers. Crack your wrists. *Y se te clavan en los pulmones.* Pull out the tubes of your organs like, um, like a dog pulls apart a toy.

Finally they reach your heart, which is still, somehow, you don't know how, it is still beating. You don't want it to. You would stop it if you could, anything, anything to stop this agony – because the worst part is – it's all your fault, you know somehow it's all your fault, for not being stronger, for not being leather and steel, for the mistakes that you made, but it's too late now because –

The hands are deep inside. They carefully grip your heart. You can feel them beginning to squeeze. At first gentle, then harder, like pressure when the carbon becomes a diamond, this pressure it turns your heart harder, until at last, you cry out, they let go –

And your heart, she just falls right out of you. Like a stone.

She says nothing.
He stares at her.

Irene What?

Manuel I was just thinking you remember me of someone.

Irene Who? Not your wife. Please don't say your wife.

Manuel Paris Hilton?

Irene Are you kidding me? I am literally nothing like Paris Hilton. I don't even look like her. What?

Manuel Who do most people remember you of?

Irene Who do I *remind* people of? (*Pause.*) I don't know. Nobody.

> *Pause.*
> *Irene casts about the room.*

Do you think I could throw on some music?

> *She runs to a stack of CDs.*

Okay. I love that you still have CDs. Who still has CDs? Welcome to Europe.

> *She puts some music on.*
> *It's upbeat and annoying.*

Manuel Wait. Stop. Let me.

> *He goes to the CDs.*
> *Looks through them.*
> *It's painful.*
> *He chooses one.*

Here. This.

> *He hands her a disc.*

Irene Okay. (*Goes to the CD player.*) Power on.

> *She puts on the CD.*
> *The music plays. It's 'O mio babbino caro', sung by Maria Callas. Manuel is utterly frozen.*
> *They listen together for a beat.*

Wait. I know this. Everybody knows this. It's in, like, a thousand commercials – what is this from? Oh yeah, it's the soundtrack to *A Room with a View*.

Manuel 'O mio babbino caro'. 'My dear father'. It's a daughter, begging for him . . . To help her marry her true love.

A beat.
They listen.

Irene It's nice.

Manuel This is what you say? Nice?

Irene Okay. Fine. What would you say?

Manuel *Que te atraviesa el corazón con la más extraordinaria belleza y te muestra el alma de la humanidad.* You can just say . . . *preciosa*.

Irene *Preciosa*. Okay. *Muy preciosa*.

Manuel Yes.

They listen.

Irene Manolo?

Manuel Manuel.

Irene Manuel?

Manuel What?

Irene (*a sudden, horrible realisation*) I just, I think this might be the most *preciosa* thing that's ever happened to me in my whole entire life.

Manuel It's okay.

Irene No, it's actually really, really sad when you think about it. No offence.

Manuel I understand.

Irene It's just you know, life back home is very, not *preciosa*. Most of the time I feel not at all *preciosa*. I mean, it's fine it's just . . . the opposite of this.

He looks at her with tenderness.

Manuel Is it all right if I . . .

Irene What?

He carefully takes her face in his hands, both of his hands, like he's memorising it.

Manuel Is it all right?

Irene Yes.

Manuel I just want to look at you.

She nods.
It's very strange and intimate.

Irene Can I just say . . . I actually do feel really connected to you, you know?

Manuel Yes.

Irene And so . . . This is not a big deal. But I just feel like maybe now's the moment when I should say that, the thing is . . . the bachelorette party is . . . It's kind of . . . mine.

He drops his hands from her face.

Manuel I know.

Irene What?

Manuel What.

Irene You *knew*?

Manuel Of course.

Irene How?

Manuel You are wearing the big diamond ring, for wedding, right?

Irene I mean, yeah but –

Manuel Also, I was watching, before you come over, the other ladies putting the shiny panties on your head.

Irene They were just being crazy.

Manuel So, I think, this must be her wedding. The one with the shiny panties.

Irene (*thinks, then*) Wait, so, what, you were like making out with me and everything, even though you *knew I was engaged?*

Manuel Yes.

Irene That's so fucked up.

Manuel You also knew you were engaged.

Irene No, I'm fucked up, that's obvious, but, I mean, part of what my life depends on is that the other people around me not, like, sink to my level.

Manuel That's not a good thing to depend on.

Irene Apparently not.

Manuel No.

Irene Anyway. The wedding's in two weeks.

Irene gets up and starts to look for her clothes.

Manuel What are you doing?

Irene I – I'm sorry – I'm stressed out, you know, I'm making bad decisions. You have to understand, it's, getting married is like a nightmare.

Manuel I thought it was fairy tale.

Irene No, no, I'm telling you it's like, it's like there's this machine, this *wedding industrial complex*.

Manuel A machine?

Irene Yeah, and the whole thing is completely overwhelming, and, and then before you know it you're in over your head and everything's so expensive and the invitations are out there, and everyone's coming and you've like picked out a dress but the tailor fucked up and so the dress makes your armpits look fat, and a cake has been ordered but you didn't know about your future mother-in-law's best friend's nut allergy and you picked out, like *dishes*, you picked out dishes and you just think, wow, you think I'm going to be eating off of these fucking dishes for a long fucking time, like when I'm too old to *chew*, I'll still be eating like mashed potatoes off these same dishes, and that's if I'm lucky, that's the good version . . . (*Thinks.*) Sometimes I fantasise that I'll die, or, like the plane will crash or something on the way home so I won't have to go through with the whole thing. I think that's probably normal, though.

The phone rings again: Beyoncé.

Shit. I thought I turned that off. I'm drunk.

Manuel So this is him? Calling?

Irene That's his ringtone. Todd.

Manuel Todd? This is name?

Irene Yeah, like Todd . . . Well, actually I can't really think of any famous Todds.

Manuel Shall I answer?

Irene No! Jesus –

It stops ringing. A long beat. It starts again: Beyoncé.

Manuel He's probably worried.

Irene You think?

The phone cuts out.
She goes to it.
Looks at it.

Shit. It's dead.

Manuel You would like to use mine?

Irene Oh. Really? Thanks.

Manuel We don't want him to worry.

Irene Right. No.

Manuel You know the number?

Irene Of course I know the number. It's my fiancé.

Manuel Ah. Right. Only dial this for US.

He hands her his phone.
  She dials.
  Listens into the phone.
  Todd answers.

Irene (*into phone*) Hi honey . . . No, it's me. Hi.
Oh, yeah, I'm fine.
No, this is the hotel phone, my phone died, so –
Sorry, yeah, just been out with the girls . . .

She looks to Manuel.

It's so fun. Yeah, lots of tapas . . .
They have the little garlic shrimp you like.
Of course, yes, tons of sangria . . .
Yeah, I'm a little, right now actually . . .
No, I'm just hanging with the girls, so . . .
No, she's not being too annoying.
I think the whole getting a dog thing, like, mellowed her . . .

She listens.
  Laughs.

No, I don't think they even have strippers in Spain . . .
Please!

Manuel looks at her: of course they have strippers in Spain.
  Irene goes to hide behind a chair, for privacy.

And that wouldn't be *my* thing anyway.
 What? No, I'm just saying . . . What?
 Yeah, I'll call you when I wake up.
 (*With real feeling.*) I miss you.
 Okay. Good night. I love you too.

*She hangs up the phone.
 Gives it back to Manuel.
 He pockets it.
 An awful pause.*

Manuel It's okay.

Irene Don't say that, please, it's not okay –

Manuel All right.

Irene No, not all right. Really not all right.

Manuel Okay.

Irene Not okay! Todd is, he's, like, a total hard-ass, like, there is no way he would understand about me hooking up with some random Spanish guy like two weeks before our wedding.

Manuel This is me. Random Spanish guy?

Irene He's a deacon at our church. He works for my dad, he's taking over the business one day. He doesn't tolerate, like, any kind of human fuck-ups – he's like my dad that way.

Manuel He sounds great.

Irene And so . . . Not that you'll ever bump into him in Denver, but just, this didn't happen, okay?

Manuel Okay.

Irene And look, it's not personal –

Manuel It's not personal? I'm a person. You are a person. It's personal.

Irene Okay – that's not what personal means – I don't think – anyway how do I get a cab? Do I need cash? (*Finding her wallet.*) Shit, I'm out of cash.

Manuel Too many sangrias / at the bar

Irene This is so like me. I always, just at the last minute, I can't, like, I 'self-sabotage', is what they call it in this book I've been reading. It's like I think I don't deserve to be happy or something.

Manuel You probably don't.

Irene What?

Manuel Nobody *deserve* to be happy.

Irene *Everybody* deserves to be happy.

Manuel Why?

Irene *Because.*

Manuel Ah. *Putos Americanos.*

Irene Okay, fine, I get it, nobody likes us, we're Americans, we're ruining the world, but you know what? It's also who I am and where I'm from and I'm proud of it, so –

Manuel You are?

Irene Of course.

Manuel Tell me. I never understand this.

Irene What?

Manuel You are proud to be American? But what did you do? Did you do anything to be American? If you were something else, would you feel shame?

Irene What's your point?

Manuel In life, you can be proud because you do something, you win a race, you write a book, you raise a child. You didn't do anything, you're just American, it makes no sense to me. 'Proud to be American.' It's luck.

Irene Yeah, but my ancestors literally walked –

Manuel Yes, they walk very far. Okay yes, but also you realise. They kill everyone in the way. This was *genocidio*, yes, genocide –

Irene Okay, seriously? Seriously? Don't even, don't even get me started on, like, the conquistadors, okay?

Manuel *Conquistadores*, yes, the difference is, I don't save the quilts.

Irene My people were fleeing religious persecution. Yours were just, like, taking shit, just like, kings and queens, just like taking whatever you wanted –

Manuel That's right, you don't take anything. You just live side by side, praying to God in peace and harmony.

Irene Well . . . I didn't do it. None of that was me.

Manuel And yet, you're proud. Ah. See what I mean?

Irene Okay, fine, forget it, and anyway, just 'cause I'm American doesn't mean I'm, like, American with a capital A. I'm a lower-case. Okay? I didn't do anything so bad – well I did tonight, but not in the grand scheme of things – and, and, the point is, *I love my fiancé.*

Manuel Okay.

Irene I do. Todd is amazing. He's just, like, a beautiful person inside and out. And yeah, maybe sometimes he's strict or – whatever – but he takes care of me. And he even sometimes does cute little things like rubs my head in front of the TV, or gives me foot massages, or, like, if I'm sick brings home soup with these cheddar cheese Goldfish crackers he knows I like and puts them in the soup and stirs and they swim around and . . .

Manuel Shhh, it's okay.

Irene (*more upset*) Like real fish, you know, they swim almost like real fish.

Manuel Cute.

Irene Yeah, because, see, that's what he calls me, his little baby goldfish, and I don't want to stop . . . (*Hard to say.*) See I don't want to stop being his little baby goldfish anymore.

Irene is weeping.
   Manuel finds a tissue for her.

Thanks.

Manuel It's all right.

Irene I don't know what's wrong with me.

Manuel Perhaps it's only the 'jet lag'.

Irene That's right. I am really jet-lagged.

Manuel It's a far trip.

Irene Yes. It's really, / really far.

Manuel And you are tired, and drunk –

Irene No, yeah, I'm just jet-lagged and, and, and drunk and I'm hungry, starving, actually, I'm fucking starving, it's lunchtime in Denver. Do you have any food here? Is there anything to eat? Or just water? I'm so fucking thirsty. And my head, my head is killing me.

Manuel I don't know what there is. Not much. Perhaps some old things in cans. Olives. Sardines. Dry salami. I suppose, if we don't eat tonight, it will all turn to dust –

Irene What will?

Manuel Everything.

Irene Oh, right. You mean. You mean because they're tearing the place down.

Manuel Yes. *Demolicion*.

Irene Demolition? Like, a wrecking ball?

Manuel Yes. Destroy it. Gone like smoke.

Irene Well . . . (*Looking around.*) I guess that's comforting.

Manuel It is?

Irene Destroy the evidence, you know? It's a relief.

Manuel Maybe it will be.

Irene Yeah.

Manuel So, perhaps we eat?

Irene I do hate to waste food.

Manuel Yes. I make you a plate.

He goes to the kitchen.
  Irene lies down on the sofa, suddenly feeling very ill.
  After a beat, she opens her eyes and starts to look around the apartment, recovering from her meltdown.

Irene It's kind of a shame they're tearing this place down. It's so cute here. It's so. Cute. (*Finds a little stuffed donkey.*) Oh, I love this little donkey. I had something just like this when I was little. Just exactly like this donkey, except it was a bear.

 I loved that bear. It was the best bear ever, and then, I lost it while we were travelling, I remember, with my parents. I was like, twelve and I think we went to London or somewhere and I lost it in the airport.

 And, you know what? Sometimes I still think of that bear, you know, this lonely traveller, like, still travelling from airport to airport, all around the world. Waiting by baggage claim. Or getting pizza at Sbarro. Shopping duty-free. Or just drinking at the airport bar.

Manuel re-enters with a plate of food.

What are you going to do with all this stuff?

Manuel I've been packaging but . . . No. (*He looks around, making a decision.*) Perhaps I let it go, up like smoke.

Irene But won't that piss her off?

Manuel Who?

Irene Whoever really lives here?

Manuel It's her fault, for leaving it.

Irene I know, I get it, you're angry, but still she's . . .

Manuel What?

Irene Never mind.

Manuel What? What? You can say.

Irene Your daughter?

He looks at her.
  Shrugs, caught.

No, don't feel bad. Look, okay, yes, it's kind of gross and embarrassing to use your kid's place as a fuckpad.

But I'm, like, so not in a place to judge you right now. And I didn't mean to pry, I just – it was obvious. It's the frilly curtains. The schoolbooks all over the place? The old lipsticks and, like, mascaras in the bathroom medicine cabinet? And plus, it's kind of a mess in here, so I knew it had to be someone young, or, like, a student?

Because, this happened to me, I was doing Habitat for Humanity one summer? And I wanted to sublet my place but I had, like, no time to pack, so my mom came over and – she was pretty pissed actually – but still, she packed everything up for me and sent it to storage, which was so totally sweet. She completely saved me. That's what parents do, I guess.

Manuel My daughter, she is same. So, how do you say, completely unresponsible – look at all these things she leave –

Irene Well, she's young –

Manuel No excuses.

Irene I'm just saying –

Manuel Stupid girl.

Irene Yeah, I understand, but –

Manuel You can't understand. Eat and then go.

He puts the food down in front of her. She starts to eat.

Irene (*quietly*) I do. I think I do understand. I think I do get it. I think you're, you're pissed at your daughter, you take it out on me.

Manuel No.

Irene That's how it works, actually, it's, it's, like, either projection or transference – I can't remember the difference right now. I took psych in college – I was actually going to be a psychologist.

Manuel Really? *Madre mia.*

Irene (*laughs, self-aware*) I know, right? Anyway, now I'm in real estate. Todd wants me to quit once we get married, but I kind of like it.

Manuel You do? This is what you love? Buying and selling –

Irene Yeah, real estate? It's like the buying and selling of homes?

Manuel Real estate, yes –

Irene Like, this place, for example, it would be so cute for the right person. Open-plan kitchen. Vaulted brick. There's a spot for everyone, that's what I like to say. It's fun to figure it out. And sometimes – no, never mind –

Manuel What?

Irene No, it's going to sound stupid –

Manuel Tell me.

Irene Okay well, there's this thing I do sometimes. I have the keys, right? To the houses. So sometimes I like to go there when nobody is home, like during the day if they both work or whatever, and I just, I go in, and I just walk around like it's my life. I brush my hair with their hairbrushes. I eat a cracker or two. I pet their cats. One time I got in the bathtub. And sometimes? I just sit on the sofa.

Manuel And?

Irene That's it.

Manuel You just sit on the sofa.

Irene For hours. Sometimes all afternoon. Or sometimes I'll, like, act like I'm talking to someone, an imaginary guest. Like I'll say, whatever, something like, don't you love my window treatments? We just had them redone! Aren't the floors fantastic? Or I'll offer someone an hors d'oeuvre. I'll be like, spanakopita? That's Greek. You know, cheese puff?

Manuel This is your fantasy? 'Cheese puffs'?

Irene You think it's dumb?

Manuel You offer imaginary cheese puffs to imaginary people?

Irene Forget it. It's just a thing I do. It's just nice to have some time away from Todd.

Manuel And you tell Todd that you do this?

Irene Why would I tell him? That would take all the fun out of it.

Manuel I don't know, he's the man that you love, maybe, maybe not –

Irene Anyway, this isn't about him. You're missing the point.

Manuel I see the point. The point is sad. / Your whole sad life –

Irene What? No, no, forget it, forget it –

Manuel It's a sad, secret life on the sofas of strangers –

Irene Okay, no, I do not – you don't / know me –

Manuel Even look at you, look at you now, where are you now?

Irene What do you mean, I'm, / I'm –

Manuel Sitting on the sofa of a stranger, eating my food, lying and cheating and running away / from your life –

Suddenly wild, out of control, and a bit terrifying, Irene grabs the wine bottle.
 With a loud, barbaric yell she pours it over her head.
 She is drenched.
 Manuel is horrified.

Irene Ooops.

Manuel What was that?!

Irene I don't know.

Manuel That was the special Rioja.

Irene I know –

Manuel You don't waste this special Rioja –

He unleashes a string of Spanish expletives.

Irene I know. I just. I'm soaked –

She runs to look for something in boxes, in the pantry, anywhere and everywhere.
 Manuel finds a dishcloth to wipe up the spilled wine.

Is there anything here I can use to get this out? Anything?

*He ignores her as she continues to look.
After a moment, the lights go out.
The apartment is suddenly flooded with orange lamplight from outside, and bright, white moonlight.*

Hey! What just happened to the lights?

Manuel They went out.

Irene Did you just do that?

Manuel Most likely they turn it off because they coming to destroy –

Irene Well, what the hell? I can't see. It's pitch black back here. How am I supposed to find anything?

A crash.

Aaaah, what the hell is that!

Manuel ignores her begins to look for a flashlight or candles.

Manuel (*to himself*) Donde . . . Donde estan estos . . . Qué es esto, no . . .

Irene (*over him, simultaneous*) Ow! I don't know what I just – oh, wait, I think I just found something, it's a . . . What is this . . . It's a Coke Light?

He is looking for candles still, in the boxes, on the shelves.

Manuel (*to himself*) Aqui, no . . .

Irene Ugh. How long has this been here? Whatever, I'm literally parched.

*She pops it open and starts to drink.
Winces at the taste.*

Okay, I'm going just borrow something to change into till this thing dries out, okay? Thanks, I'm just, this thing is totally drenched, so . . . I'll be right back.

Irene grabs something from a box, disappears into the bathroom.
Manuel barely notices, as he begins to light the candles.
Suddenly the whole room looks romantic, or shrine-like.
He pauses to take it in and lights a cigarette for himself.
He smokes.
Now Irene appears in the doorway wearing the dress.

It fits.

Manuel turns to look at her.
He freezes.

I guess we're the same size.

For a long moment, Manuel can't speak.

Manuel Put up your hair.

Irene Why?

Manuel Only because it is dripping wine drops on the dress.

Irene Oh.

Manuel Her favourite.

Irene Oh. Sure.

She puts up her hair.

How's this?

Manuel Perfect.

He pauses, taking solace in the sight.

Irene Huh. Okay. Well. Do you mind if I . . .

She starts back to the bathroom.

Manuel No, please, just . . . Be still.

Irene I –

Manuel Shhh. Don't talk. Please.

A long beat of silence.
Manuel circles her slowly, as if trying to see her from the right angle.
Irene doesn't dare talk or move.

Don't be afraid. Are you afraid?

Irene No no no.

Manuel Don't be scared.

Irene I'm not. I'm not scared.

Manuel Good.

He approaches her with an eerie gentleness.
She is trembling.
She suddenly bolts for the door.

No! Don't go –

He lunges at her, grabs her –
She bites him, gets free –
They grapple ferociously –

Irene Let go of me –

Manuel *La vestido –*

Irene Get off –

Manuel *Dame el vestido –*

Irene Let go, get off me, get away –

Irene desperately tries to get to the door.

(*Kicking, scratching her way free.*) I can't help you – I don't know what you want from me – I'm not – your daughter –

In the fight, the dress rips –
   Manuel stops pursuing Irene, curls up on the floor, holding the fabric. In deep pain.
   Irene stops. Stares at him. The dress.

Irene I'm sorry. It can be . . . mended.

Manuel It cannot be mended.

   Pause.

Irene Your daughter. She's . . .

   He looks at her.

I'm sorry. I'm so sorry.

   Pause.

Manuel Sofia.

Irene Sofia.

   Pause.

How did she – no, not that, it's not any of my – it doesn't matter.

Manuel Of course, it matters. When someone is gone, everything matters.

Irene Right, that's not what I meant, I just meant . . . If you don't want to talk about it . . .

   Manuel looks up at her.

Manuel We already talk about it.

Irene We . . .

Manuel Atocha station.

Irene The . . . She was killed . . . in the bombing?

Manuel Because of your war.

Irene Not my war.

Pause.
He shakes his head.

Manuel The day before, tenth of March, it's my birthday, I tell her, come, stay the day with me –

Irene Right, but you couldn't have known –

Manuel The next day, she must get back here to class, in Barcelona – of course, she cannot go to university near home, where I work – no, this was her, always making everything fucking complicated. She ask me to drive her to Atocha, I tell her no, I'm too tired, you're grown up, come on, take the train. If I drive her, she would still be alive, today.

Irene That doesn't make it your fault.

Manuel I say goodbye. I go back to bed. Stupid. I'm asleep when it happens. Sleeping, when this happens to my girl.

Irene takes that in with empathy.

I wake up, I see this on the news. I call her phone right away. Just the message. I find my wife, she's in the shower –
 I say – Sofia's not answering her phone.
 We get in the car. The whole time, silence in the car. I drive, my wife just keeps dialling. Dialling the phone. I can feel her thinking, it's my fault, why did I not drive – but we don't say a word.
 I am hoping perhaps Sofia is just – no consciousness, unconscious – she got knocked from the blast, she will wake up and see one hundred calls from us and she will laugh at us later. She was always making fun of us like this. We always worried too much.
 When we get to Atocha, it was . . .

He shakes his head: it's indescribable.

They ask us what . . . (*Very hard to say.*) What clothes she had on.

Manuel is overcome for a moment.

I apologise. I never . . .

Irene It's okay.

Pause.

Manuel They take us into a large room.

Like a, a waiting room. I see that they are taking the people in through one door, but taking them out another way. I understand this is because . . .

They don't want anyone to come back into the waiting room to speak of what they have seen.

We wait. It feels forever. The silence of the room. The silence of my phone.

And any moment I'm thinking, this is so silly, at any moment, Sofia will come through the door of the station. We will all go home for lunch. Or more likely, she will convince me to drive her all the way to Barcelona. She hates to miss class.

At last, they take us into the room. A great room. The bodies, laid out, over one hundred.

My wife looks very calm, very sure, and says . . . Isn't that strange. There is a girl here, and she is wearing the exact same dress as Sofia. But it's not her – *no es Ella*.

But it was.

Irene is at a loss for words.

Irene What was she like?

Manuel Brown eyes. Long hair. She would put it up, for parties. She was learning Italian cooking. She was a terrible cook. She liked football, the real kind. She loved Raúl, you know who this is? Raúl? From Real Madrid? No?

Irene No.

Manuel No. She was . . . very . . . kind. Very nice.

Irene *Preciosa*.

Manuel Yes. She was always doing these stupid, nice things – like, one time, she find some baby mice in the park? She package them in her, her backpack and takes them home. Into our house.

Irene Oh no.

Manuel My wife opens the bag of mice, she almost had a heart attack, right? My daughter, she said, 'What was I supposed to do? Leave them to die?' Stupid nice, you see?

Irene Yeah.

Manuel She wanted to get married. A big wedding, with all her friends. She didn't even have a boyfriend! But she wants this big wedding with dancing like, she would always dance like this *Saturday Night Fever* –

Irene John Travolta.

Manuel Yes. Every time music was on, she would dance that way.

Irene She sounds wonderful.

He stares at Irene.

Manuel And this is only why, you see. When I notice you at the bar. Her favourite bar. I think only, I can only think, why are these girls, these stupid girls, I'm sorry to say it like this –

Irene No, it's all right –

Manuel Why are they here and Sofia is not? Why is she, that one, why is she getting married? Why is she alive, see, when my daughter is not?

He looks at her with rage and sadness.
Irene has no words.

Irene (*simple, honest*) I don't know.

Manuel Okay. At least this is true.

Irene Yes.

Pause.
He stares at her.

What?

Manuel It's only I think, I just realise the thing you remember me of.

Irene Her?

Manuel No.

Irene Right.

Manuel Only there is something, this part is the same: her life was stolen from her. Yours, you throw it away.

Irene What are you . . .

Manuel I have been listening to you all night. You talk and you talk and you talk.

Irene I know.

Manuel You are living a life you don't like. You are marrying a man you don't love.

Irene (*searching for words*) I . . .

Manuel You destroy your life.

Irene Well, no, it's not, it's not, not on purpose. I mean, what else am I / supposed to do –

Manuel And this, after everything, this is not something I can accept. It is a tragedy to lose your life. It is shameful to waste it.

Manuel goes to his phone, picks it up.

Irene What are you doing?

Manuel Here, this is him, most recent dialled –

Irene Whoa, okay, what are you – / okay wait, no, okay, wait, what are you doing –

Manuel Only tell him the truth, that you don't love him –

Irene What?!

Manuel That you go home with a Spanish stranger –

Irene No, okay, whoa, no, he'd never understand, he'd never forgive me –

Manuel Good.

Irene Why are we even talking about me? We were talking about your daughter –

Manuel You are here. She is not.

Irene Okay, but look, I, I . . . Okay. I know it's . . . I know how it seems, this, my whole, situation . . .

Manuel Yes.

Irene And I appreciate your concern, but – you just, you have to believe me –

Manuel What?

Irene There's nothing I can do.

Manuel Nothing you can do? No, you can do something.

Irene No, you have to understand – my parents and everyone at home – they would hate me – forever –

Manuel So?

Irene So I'll have nobody – and nothing and – I know it sounds silly or stupid or weak – maybe I'm not that strong –

Manuel Strong like bull?

Irene Right, no, actually, no because – I know it seems bad but – this is all I have – this is what I've signed up for – and so, it's not perfect, maybe – but I'll be okay. And anyway, I just . . . I can't change it right now – I just . . . can't.

Manuel Let's see.

Manuel stares at her a beat.
  He presses dial on the phone.

Irene What are you doing?

Through the phone, the sound of ringing.

Manuel I can tell him, if it's easier –

Irene No, are you crazy, please, stop, stop it, no, I . . . I can't do it, I can't, I can't, I can't, I . . .

Manuel Try. Be brave.

Todd (*muffled, half-audible, from the phone*) Hello? Hello?

Irene takes the phone.

Irene Todd?
  Todd, yeah, hi? Hi, um, it's me.
  Yep, hi, it's me, it's your little baby goldfish.

How did . . . How did the meeting go?
  Oh, it's tomorrow? Wait, I'm so confused.

Am I . . . No, well, good question because, no, I'm not all right.
  I'm really not all right, I . . . I'm in Spain.
  Well, actually Catalunya, it's a whole different . . .
  Anyway. You know that. That's not important right now.

Todd?

She looks to Manuel for a long beat.

There's something I should tell you.
  This is no big deal but . . .

She takes a deep breath.

I'm not at the hotel.
 I'm with . . .
 A man.

Well, because I went back to his place and . . .
 Nothing really happened, we just talked, really . . .
 Well that's not true, we didn't just talk but . . .
 Honestly . . .
 It didn't mean anything.

Ashamed, she tries not to look at Manuel.

I was just drunk. Really drunk.
 I didn't know what I was doing . . .
 I was completely out of my mind.
 I was really, really . . .
 Yeah, I'm still, I'm with him now.

No, Todd, don't call the cops, don't call the cops, it's fine, he's fine, he's not –
 No, Todd, please, don't just –
 Stop.
 Listen to me.
 Please.
 I'm okay.

You know I think it's just that self-sabotage thing that we talked about?
 That I do sometimes?
 Like on the driver's test when I suddenly, you know, forgot how to park the car?
 Stupid, I know.
 You're right.
 Or maybe it's . . .
 Maybe it's . . .
 I don't know.
 I'm an idiot.
 Yeah.
 It could be as simple as that.

Todd? Do you think you can ever forgive me?

A beat. She listens. Exhales in relief.

Oh. Oh, Todd, thank you.
    Yeah, I'll come right home.
    Oh, I don't deserve you, seriously Todd.
    I don't. Thank you.

She looks at Manuel, victorious.

I think it's really just the jet lag, you know?
    I think the jet lag is really messing with my head.
    So yeah,
    I'll just come home . . .

She shuts her eyes tight.
    About to take the hardest leap of her life.

Todd?
    I don't think I can come home.
    Not now.
    Maybe not ever.

Pause.

Because Todd, I love you . . .
    But . . . The truth is . . .
    I think I might not love you.

I . . .
    I don't love you.

At least not in the way that I should.
    I might not even like you –

The point is –
    Something's missing.
    No, not from you . . .
    From us, from this, from everything –
    Something's missing in me.
    And –

The line goes dead.

Todd?
　Todd? Are you there? Todd?

*She hangs up the phone.
　Looks at Manuel.
　In a state of utter shock.*

He hung up.

Manuel It's okay.

Irene starts to laugh, almost hysterical at what's happened.

Irene He hung up . . . He . . . I . . . I'm not . . . I'm . . . Not . . .

She starts to fall apart.

What did I do, what did I just do, what am I going to do . . .

Manuel Shhh. You'll be okay. You're young.

Irene I'm not that young. Do you know how old I am? I'm not telling you how old I am.

Manuel Twenty-six? Twenty-eight?

Irene *Thirty-five.*

Manuel No.

Irene Yes.

Manuel No, I can't *believe* this. (*Pause.*) You look good.

Irene I stay out of the sun.

Manuel Ah.

Irene I don't even know – I mean what have I even done with my life? What am I doing? I can't even speak Spanish. I studied it for *four years* in high school. My ancestors walked across the country? I can't get back to my hotel without my stupid iPhone.

Manuel It's okay. You're a tourist.

Irene No, but that's what I'm saying. That's what I'm saying. I . . . I'm a tourist everywhere, all the time. I say I'm proud of America? I don't know America. I'm proud of my ancestors? They were probably terrible – they did terrible things – I don't even know what they did. And do I try to find out? No, no, I feed fake people fake cheese and talk about nothing. I'm a tourist . . . in my own life.

Manuel All I know is this. You cannot marry a man who ate a banana out of a stripper's hoo-ha.

Irene Well, that's true.

Irene almost smiles at that.

I feel like, I hope this is okay to say . . .

Manuel What?

Irene I feel like you must have been a really great dad.

Manuel No.

Irene Yes. You were. You are, why am I saying 'were', you are –

Manuel My daughter dies five years ago. You realise.

Irene I know.

Manuel So, for five years, this apartment, I keep it. Just like this. I come to visit. I stare at the walls. I sit on the sofa. I try to forget. I try to move on. Or just to . . . move. And now today, the last day comes. And still, I cannot do it. Her own father. I let her die and –

Irene It wasn't / your fault –

Manuel I let her die. And now . . . this last day comes. I cannot even pack her things.

Irene I can do it.

Manuel No.

Irene I can help you pack. I'll pack all of her things.

Manuel No, please –

Irene The movers are coming – what time did you say?

Irene goes to the window.

There are workers already out there.

Manuel Oh, are they already there?

Outside, dawn is breaking.

Irene There's a crane – with a – with the, with the –

Manuel The wrecking ball.

Irene It's already there?

Manuel It has been there, yes, already –

Irene But what time did you say that they're –

Manuel Who can tell? Perhaps soon. You should probably go.

Irene But I have to pack –

Manuel No, just leave it alone –

Irene But everything will be lost –

Manuel I don't care –

Irene No, I'm doing it.

Manuel I said forget it –

Irene But I want to –

Manuel No, it's too much –

Irene I can do it.

Manuel Please / don't –

Irene Do you want to save / everything or –

Manuel Please stop, don't –

Irene Or just the –

Manuel Stop. Please. JUST STOP. Please leave now. Please.

Irene What about you?

He looks away.
She understands.

(*Quietly.*) Someone will find you.

Manuel Inspection was yesterday.

Irene And no movers are coming.

Manuel No.

Irene Still. You can't . . .

Manuel Destroyed in the blast. Like my daughter. It's better this way.

Irene But . . .

Outside, some sounds of workmen.
Construction vehicles moving.

Manuel I want to spend this last time with her. I will be with her soon. This I know. Please respect what I want. That is all.

Irene Of course. I . . . I understand. I understand. I'll just . . .

Pause.
Irene starts to reaassemble herself.

I think I need . . . My clothes? And my other shoe. I know, I know, I threw it at your head –

Manuel I picked it up.

He produces the shoe from his coat pocket. Hands it to her.

Irene Well . . . You could have told me that. Thanks. Thank you.

Irene goes into the bathroom to change.
  Manuel sits. Smokes.
  He takes in everything in the apartment.
  He unpacks whatever might be in the boxes. He settles in.
  Sounds of construction.
  At last, she re-enters, in her original clothes, steady on both shoes.
  She looks at him.

You stay. I stay.

He stares at her.

Manuel What?

Irene I'm not leaving you here. I won't leave you alone.

Manuel Of course you will, / what are you talking –

Irene I won't, no, I'm not going to leave –

Manuel Come on, stop this, it's silly –

Irene It's not silly, I'm not silly and I'm not leaving / here –

Manuel Enough, get out / of this place – go –

Irene No, I'm sorry, I can't –

Manuel Why not –

Irene You ruined my life.

Manuel I saved your life.

Irene Well, exactly.

He stares at her.

Manuel *Ay, mujer estúpida, qué te pasa* –

Irene I don't care what you say about me – I don't / care –

Manuel Who do you think you are –

Irene Nobody, this isn't / about me –

Manuel You think you are some kind of a hero?

Irene No, that's not what I'm doing, this has / nothing to do –

Manuel It won't matter, what you do / it will not matter if you die with me –

Irene You don't decide what matters, you don't get to decide / that for me –

Manuel I am only telling you I'm finished, nothing –

Irene I don't believe you –

Manuel And I don't want you here.

Irene I think you do –

Manuel / I don't –

Irene Nobody wants to die alone.

Manuel Stop that, what do you know about anything –

Irene Isn't that why you let me come here?

Manuel Stop, / no, you have no right, you have no right – stop –

Irene Take me down with you, that was the plan, well, I'm here now, I'm here and I'm not –

Manuel Just go. (*Screams, fully enraged, a howl of pain and a roar.*) GO.

The force of his release almost knocks them both to the ground.
   He crumbles, emotion overtaking him, a lost child.

Irene (*gently*) No.

He takes that in.
  The finality of it.
  She looks around.

Anyway, the truth is . . . It's not like I was particularly looking forward to facing whatever's left of my life back in Denver.

She stops, looks out the window.

It's too bad, though. I did kind of want to see that thing.

He looks at her.

You know, the, um . . . Out the window.

Manuel The cathedral. La Sagrada Familia.

Irene It's listed as a top attraction. You know, in the guidebook. They said it's can't miss. Five stars. It's, like, the thing to do in Barcelona.

Manuel Then you should go.

Irene And you know, it's not even finished? I read this in the guidebook. It was started like over a hundred years ago and it won't be finished for another twenty-five at least, and probably not even then. It's taking forever.

Manuel Fucking Europeans.

Irene Right? But they said in the guidebook, that's part of the point. They called it a 'monument to perseverance'. You must have seen it a hundred times.

Manuel (*quietly, an admission*) I've never been to there.

Irene You've never been inside.

Manuel No.

Irene You've never been to the, like, biggest attraction in Barcelona?

Manuel No.

Irene Well. That's seems like a shame.

A pause.

Manuel What would we do?

Irene Look around. Light a candle. Pray. Have breakfast? Is there anywhere to eat around there?

Manuel There's a McDonald's right across the street.

Irene No. Really?

Manuel It's true.

Irene That's terrible!

Manuel I know. (*Pause.*) But, you know . . . It's sometimes delicious.

Irene (*laughing*) Are you kidding me? / You have got to be kidding me. You are ridiculous –

Manuel I said sometimes, some things, no, listen, I still think it's terrible, but it can be delicious.

Their laughter begins to subside a little.

Irene Like life, I guess.

Manuel Like life.

Irene picks up the little donkey.
Considers it.

Irene So, what's the protocol here? When the wrecking ball comes. Do we, like, hug, or hold hands, or –

Manuel God, you're annoying. Do you know that?

Irene Yeah. I think that should be blatantly obvious by now.

Manuel I don't even like you.

Irene You don't even know me.

Manuel True.

Irene Irene.

Manuel (*pointed*) Manuel.

Irene Got it.

> *She offers her hand.*
> *Shaking, he stands up.*
> *He slowly gets his coat.*
> *Puts it on.*
> *Buttons it.*
> *Irene looks at him, unsure.*

Vamos?

Manuel *Vamos.*

Irene That means, 'Let's go.'

> *He looks around the apartment one last time.*

Manuel I know what it means.

> *He slowly walks to the door and opens it for Irene.*
> *Together, they go out.*
> *End of play.*